Focus on the Master, Not the Messenger
by Jennifer Jo Bingham

Printed in the United States of America

ISBN 978-0-615-62178-4

Unless otherwise indicated, Bible quotations are taken from the New King James Version (http//:blueletterbible.org).

February 2013

Focused on the Master

Not the Messenger

Jennifer Jo Bingham

Dedication

This 2013 release is dedicated to Alexis (know that in the midst of any crowd, no matter how large God will always see you. You will never be lost to Him) and to CrIcKo (my life would still be on "pause" had we never crossed paths. Thanks for finding my keys).

This book is dedicated to SELA, my little soldiers who held my arms up through the battle (keeping me quite tickled along the way) and to my dad, I miss you love you always; to my "coach" Doreen and Joseph Samsa whose passion for a Christ-filled life has to this day, in my life, been unparalleled, for their love, friendship and encouragement beyond words; to Ray and Barbara Llamas for words of wisdom that have echoed in my mind through the years and have proven to be priceless; to my "Red Wire" for the part you played in bringing music to my soul, not to mention the laughter and joy; to my fellow "Diplomat" for helping me begin what would be an incredible journey, for that "I gotchur' back".

I also dedicate this book to our incredible and growing team at Inspire the Fire, it is an honor to work with such inspiring people with such an amazing heart for the Lord; to James and Tami Marti for their friendship, counsel and example, thanks for always pushing; to Kevin Rhodes for helping me, through his testimony, to keep my focus on Christ when I needed it most; and last but never least, to my husband, the wonder twins and KEDWE, I love you all!

I am only one person. I cannot begin to imagine how many lives you have touched. Thank you!

Jennifer Jo Bingham

Table of Contents

Once Upon a Time – a testimony of sorts

Once upon a time I was a child with dreams,
A child with hope beyond what could be seen.
A child who dared to believe with the heart
What the world had to offer would just be the start.
I had to look deeper than what I saw with my eyes.
It was then the Lord helped me realize
I was made for His glory and His glory alone.
He looked down on this child and called me His own.
He drew me in close and then closer still.
Such a tender young age, yet he showed me His will.
He taught me what others take a lifetime to learn;
He loves me so much that one day He'll return.
And while I'm here waiting, there's much work to do
And I'm someone He's chosen to do that work through.

Once upon a time, along the road I traveled
All of my hopes and dreams unraveled.
I lost sight of the child who once dared to believe;
Confused, disillusioned and with a heart that grieved.
All of the heartache and constant rejecting
Wasn't the life I'd been expecting.
I didn't sign up for a world this cold.
It had become much worse than what I'd been told.
I had forgotten the lessons I had learned as a child
I forgot how to focus and my heart ran wild.
I needed to stop living life in despair
And my own perspective is what kept me there.
How could I be used as a tool for His glory
When all I could see was a sad life's story?

Once upon a time I gave up on my plans
And placed them in the palms of God's hands.
I surrendered my life and all that I was
And everything changed that moment because…
Because everything changes when Christ is involved.
Life didn't stop but the sorrows dissolved.
All of a sudden the hurt from the past
Became an experience that was meant to last.
Not just something to be hidden and buried
But a gift to help others release burdens they've carried.
I no longer look back and see a sad life story
But rather a tool to be used for God's glory.
He's able to use disappointments and strife
To give us the strength for a victorious life!

My Race to the Starting Line

Usually when we think of a race, the end goal is to reach the "finish line" and rightly so. However, so many of us never even enter the race because we simply "don't know where to begin." But determining where that starting line begins for you is a journey that you alone can make and it is not something that others can push you towards (no matter how hard they may try). You alone will know when the time is right.

I've always known I was running the good race but I was so focused on the finish line that I didn't pay quite as much attention to my surroundings as I probably should have. I felt the sore muscles (heartaches) and (emotional) exhaustion. I've felt the desperate longing for it (life) all to be over with but I continued on through sheer determination. And there it was… I could hear the crowd cheering me on as I eagerly approached. It was then that the reality of what just happened began to dawn on me, as I read that great big banner now facing me; "START."

Now, you can probably imagine my response to be something along the lines of, "What?! You've got to be kidding...start? That's supposed to be the finish line! No way! I give up, this is ridiculous"… but you would be wrong. You see, as sore and exhausted as I had been when I approached that starting line, it was all forgotten as I took in the new surroundings. What an arena! It was the difference between running a track meet at the middle school level and having the opportunity to run for Olympic gold! All of a sudden, my energy was replenished and my previously sore muscles were now flexing in anticipation. Instead of longing for a collapse, I couldn't wait for the shot to go off. This was my moment, my chance to reach for the highest goal (Philippians 3:14). And boy, was I ready!

As all Olympic runners know, you have to come across a lot of starting lines before you can finally compete at such an intense level. How many? I don't know. It will differ from person to person. Just don't lose heart. When I thought I was already in the race, I was still only in training. I wasn't yet ready for the competition. God was refining my skill (knowledge and wisdom), conditioning my body (spirit) and exercising my muscles (faith and perseverance). Now, just because I can see the track and have some sort of direction, that does not mean He has finished with me. There is still much work to be done but He who began the good work will be faithful to complete it (Philippians 1:6). And there is no greater coach than the Creator of the universe! With God at our side, the victory is guaranteed! We are more than conquerors for the victory has already been won (Romans 8:37/1 John 5:4).

Therefore we also, since we are surrounded by so great a cloud of witnesses, let us lay aside every weight, and the sin which so easily ensnares us, and let us run with endurance the race that is set before us,– Hebrews 12:1

The Treasure in the Testimony
I Failed To Share

I hesitate as I begin this chapter. These pages are not filled with the story of a bright beginning. But neither is it as foreboding as some of the topics which will be touched upon. Remember, the title of this book is Focused on the Master, Not the Messenger. So please do not focus on the people or events that are presented but rather, focus on how God moved through them (Romans 8:28). Focus on how God is able to reach hearts with an eternal touch despite them. God is so much greater than any of our circumstances. He is also more powerful than anyone person's story. So when you read these pages, be sure that the story you are focusing on is not mine – but His.

I was a child who found faith at an early age. But that wasn't the only thing I found. I also found something that no child should ever find. I learned at an early age what it was like to be abused by a loved one. And to make matters worse, at the hands of the very one who taught me the most about the love of Christ, obviously not by example. Understandably, it is not a place I like to go back to and I lived my younger years in the silence of that secret. I told no one. In the years to come, I would mention it only to people I would minister to and even then it was so quickly brushed upon you would think I was talking about the weather. I don't know why I even bothered. By minimizing the severity of the crime, I didn't just minimize my own experience but I had I minimized theirs as well.

Why then, should I mention it now? Because it's about time I did. You see, there is more than one lesson to be learned by my early experiences, both with man and with God. When I was younger I thought my experiences to be quite unique but I as I grew I began to learn differently.

It's amazing how much of the same ugliness occurs within the body of Christ and yet is never talked about. And why would we? It ruins the pretty picture we work so hard to paint to represent the Church. And I completely understand, for I am equally guilty of doing the same; not just in my early years but in my adult years as well. But it makes me wonder if perhaps there would be fewer occurrences of these crimes within the church if we knew we were to be held accountable for them, as opposed to relying on the hush-hush of our cover-ups that have become almost a guarantee. How can we as a church ever be free of such demons (or strongholds) if we refuse to acknowledge them in our presence? Jesus called them out by name – why can't we? Just a thought. I knew I was not the only child who had suffered abuse. I just wasn't aware that others had the same twisted message of salvation and affliction delivered to them by a similar messenger; a double agent if you will – one person with two opposing messages. It was at that early age however, that by God's grace alone, I learned to separate the sins of man from the love and will of God.

Just recently I was talking to a friend of mine. This was someone who also had a history of childhood abuse which later led her down a road of self-inflicted abuse. That was before Christ came into her life in a new and powerful way and set her free. We had both been invited to speak at a Christian youth conference in Florida but she was having doubts on whether or not she should go. During one of our phone conversations it was revealed that the reason she did not want to go was because she was going to give her testimony and the person who had violated her all those years ago was going to be in the audience. She didn't want him to be hurt. He was going to the event to support her at this speaking engagement but once he found out that she would be giving her testimony, his support began to falter. He no longer had peace about it in his spirit and told her that it wasn't of God.

I reassured her that her testimony would be a powerful tool to reach out to a lot of hurting souls, not to mention it would be a great growth experience for her by taking such a step of boldness for the Lord. She should keep in mind though that the offending party was never going to feel peace in his spirit regarding the role he played in her testimony. Yet it should also be noted that if he had come to a point in his life where he was willing to support her in ministry, then some significant healing had obviously taken place in that relationship. What she could do to make it less awkward was tell her testimony without naming the "who" that was the offender. If it was handled in this manner, he would not feel as though people were looking at him in disgust, especially when he had already repented and been forgiven of his sins. I was also sure to remind her that anything she would have to say would be of no surprise to him. He was already aware of the hurt it had caused them both. Besides, after so many years of carrying this dark secret (protecting something that did not protect her), it was about time to let go of that burden. And the truth will set her free (John 8:36).

She agreed that it would be a good way to approach the situation and still be sensitive to all parties involved. But there was one more thing holding her back and this was the worst news of all. In fact, it is the reason I decided to write this book and address the issue in the first place. My dear friend had begun to doubt her own relationship with God. This is perhaps the most dangerous side effect of receiving the message of salvation by a "double agent" (one who serves God in one moment and becomes a tool for Satan in the next). You see, she had been taught about her faith by the same person who had abused her. And because of that she began to wonder if her belief was really her faith at all. What if it was just the his faith that had been shoved down her throat and that she had no true relationship with God at all? I could hear the desperateness in her voice as she expressed her doubts. She said she couldn't explain it but sometimes, out of nowhere, those thoughts would plague her. My spirit was deeply troubled by this but fortunately, the storms that I had weathered early on in my life had prepared me to speak into hers…

I told her we shared similar beginnings but that the important part was to remember that God and man are not the same. God could have used an unbeliever to reach us if He chose to. It doesn't matter which vessel He uses to call us to Him (good or bad). The important thing is that He calls us. It's a shame that it happened the way it did but we should not credit the person, the sermon, or the song, (etc.) that brought us to Christ for our relationship with Christ. Instead we can be grateful that God was able to use them at all. But remember, they are only the source. What we do with the knowledge of that salvation and how we nurture that relationship with Christ is ours and ours alone. And as for how those thoughts seem to appear from out of nowhere… that's a sure sign that they are not of God. There are times in our lives when we will be stressed and overwhelmed because its life and we are stressed and overwhelmed. But if it comes out of nowhere and seemingly for no reason, then it is a mere tactic of the enemy, for our God is not the author of confusion but has come to bring us peace and a sound mind (1 Corinthians 14:33a/2 Timothy 1:7).

I have always been aware that God must have had a protective hedge around my mind at that tender young age. I can remember God's presence in my life long before I even knew what to call Him. And oddly enough the memories of those experiences with God are always of the same house where the abuse took place. I remember there was this painting on the wall of an angel watching over two small children as they crossed over some old, deteriorating bridge in a dark and stormy scene. It made me wonder what they were doing all alone in such a dark and scary place. Yet even then, I was already learning that sometimes… it just happens. That painting hung on the wall above where I would sleep. And all I ever really remember of those awful moments was that I would stare at that painting and know that God was watching over me. And I knew that He would get me through this dark and scary place, just as He was doing for those children in the painting. Afterwards, when I was once again alone and couldn't sleep, I would talk to the Lord until I slipped off into a peaceful rest that only He could bring (Psalm 4:8). I found my Best Friend, Jesus, at the earliest of ages and for that I am grateful.

As confusing as mixed messages go, I did not despise the talks of faith that took place in that house. On the contrary, I welcomed them. The more I learned of the life of Jesus, the closer I felt to Him. I used to love hearing about the book of Revelation because it promised His return. And interestingly enough, I learned that if I initiated those talks at night just before bedtime, by asking just the right questions, the talks would last until about 3a.m. Not only would I be filled with wonder at my God but I was also saved from abuse on those nights, as the double-agent would have enough sense (or rather, conviction) to go straight to sleep after such a long talk about the things of the Lord.

It was still a scary time, unsure if I would be safe or not, waiting for him to call it a night, hating that I was in this position but grateful it was not my little sister who was also there, sound asleep. No, I will never understand why I went through that but it allowed me to learn that God is God, despite of how man may represent Him. I learned that my relationship with God was something so pure that it could not be touched or defiled by man. It was mine and mine alone. And the more I learned about Him (literally), the more He came to my rescue. I know that was a bit ironic but it has held true throughout my entire life. Draw near to Him and He will draw near to you (James 4:8a). I also learned the power of forgiveness, which is not a weakness but a strength. And lately I have learned the importance of sharing your story, even those stories that you spent a lifetime refusing to identify with or those that you just don't believe there is any point in sharing (they were so long ago and you are "sooo over them").   It wasn't until decades later that I was able to find the treasure in the testimony I failed to share.

Was it worth revisiting? Absolutely! If I were to go back and describe the abuse alone, it would seem as though I were telling the story of another person's life, someone I no longer knew. And because of that, sometimes I feel like I can't relate to it at all; as if I "don't qualify" as a victim because I have survived so victoriously.

On the other hand, when I retell the story of how my Best Friend was always there and how He strengthened my mind and my spirit and came to my rescue, I can remember that intimacy with God so vividly. And more importantly, I continue to feel it. On those days when the enemy would come and bring doubt of God's purpose or presence in my life, I would begin to trace back all the undeniable experiences I have shared with Him. And without fail, the earliest traces are rooted back so many years ago during a time in my life that until recently, I chose to deny. And to think how often God has used those times to remind me of how He chose me and took the time to introduce Himself, right from the beginning. That knowledge and those moments of Divine intimacy have pulled me through so many barriers and over so many obstacles, to bring me to the place I am now. And they will continue to take me to the place that God has intended for me (Jeremiah 29:11).

I may have been robbed of my innocence at a young age but what I gained was something no one could ever take away. I was blessed with a close relationship with my Lord, Jesus Christ. And He would walk beside me for the rest of my life. There are others who have been through so much worse and have had so much less. I consider myself more than blessed. Thank You Jesus!

-2-
A Thousand Reasons and None

Despite having a rocky start, I still consider myself to have had a normal childhood. Or at least what seemed to be normal. My parents were married with 2.5 kids; myself, my brother and my sister (she gets the .5 for being 4 years younger). I excelled in pretty much all I did. I was accomplished in school, sports and arts. I grew up with a good head on my shoulders, a drive for success and a belief that anything was attainable. It seemed the world was mine for the conquering and the earlier events of my life seemed to be just a bleep on the radar.

But was that normal? Who determines that? Experts of abuse will say that there are certain "normal" responses to abuse; some victims will become self-destructive, some become introverted and try to draw the least bit of attention to themselves while others will become overachievers, always seeking approval and then of course, there are other stereo types in between. These are normal responses? It sounds to me that any or all responses have a place on that spectrum. So does that mean I was merely a product of my abuse? I think not. It seems to me that the traits they covered apply to everyone, regardless of whether or not they've had a history of abuse. We all fall somewhere on that spectrum so of course they are bound to hit their mark. I am not trying to undermine their wisdom or research as it has helped many, myself included. I am just saying that there is more to it than that and if people are not mindful of that then they may begin to define themselves by the negative influences in their lives and not the positive. People like to wrap things up in pretty little boxes that are easy to explain (even when there is no definite explanation). But I know differently. You may have been caught in a cycle of abuse... but your identity shouldn't be.

I was more a product of a father who was driven to succeed and installed the belief that I could do anything I wanted and become whatever I wanted to be; that no dream was out of reach. I was the product of a mother who knew how to pick her battles and let go of that which she could not control. She taught me that if I could imagine it, then it could happen, even if that meant I had to create it myself. I was also a product of the Word of God. I didn't go to church regularly until I was 14 years old but I read my Bible, prayed and jumped on the church-mobile with my grandparents at every opportunity. So it was a melting pot of all those philosophies and ways of life that have made me who I am today.

And yet there is still much to be said about the research of abuse, especially in regards to its cycle. It does repeat itself. Although who I was inside was a product of positive influences, there seemed to be this unexplainable attraction to unhealthy relationships. But it wasn't because I didn't believe I deserved more and it wasn't because I wasn't a strong and confident young woman. It was due to a thousand reasons and none. Allow me to explain… and then… unexplain.

When I was 14 years old, my family and I had gone to a baby dedication at a local church. Both my mom and I took an immediate liking to the church. While I began trying to find my own way to plug in, my mom was finding hers as well. She started helping the pastor with some administrative duties and I soon began my first ministry; cleaning bathrooms, polishing pews and working the projector during praise and worship. And thus, we found our place at my first home church.

About a year later, I met the young man who would later become my husband. His father was the pastor of the Spanish ministry at the church. By that time, I had already begun teaching in children's church and singing on the worship team. Soon I would even be asked to lead the youth group. I was grateful for the opportunity but I was still a youth myself and it was sometimes a difficult position to be in. In any case, I was ministry driven. My life was completely focused on school, sports and ministry. I didn't have time for boys nor did I wish to. But my future husband had other plans. I was later told by his friends and parents that he had prayed for me for 2 years straight and bought me a gift each week (which stayed accumulating in the trunk of his car). I was completely unaware of his interest for those two years until I began to attend the home bible studies he taught.

I was flattered by his interest but was never attracted to him. And yet I found myself marrying the man. Why? I was drawn to the Spirit within him, the passion for ministry, and the heart that sought God so intensely. I had never met anyone close to my age with the same drive as I had. I always felt "different". So there was that similar connection that came at a time when there was strife at home. Mom went to an inpatient hospital in search of her "inner child" and left me at home to take care of the house, dinners and Dad. It was too much for me and I resented her for it (and for going out with friends to dance and drink in the years before, leaving us at the home where the abuse took place) for years to come. I hated all the negative energy that was surfacing, Mom complaining about Dad, Dad complaining about Mom, grandparents talking about the threat of divorce, my brother fighting with my dad and vice versa. It was not a great time to be at home and I sought every opportunity to occupy myself in activities outside the home. But soon that wasn't enough and I was consumed with thoughts of running away. And in my own way, I did… I got married.

Now there were so many ways I could have handled that. The obvious being that I could have gone away to college instead but I didn't. And I don't blame my parents for anything either. They are just as human as the rest of us and were dealing with their own problems as best they could. I could have responded in many (many, many, many) other ways but for my own misguided reasons, I chose marriage. I talked myself into it. With exception to his love of God and ministry, he was everything I wasn't looking for. I don't say that in a condescending manner but if I had painted a picture of my ideal husband, he would have been outside the frame – our worlds were too different. But I told myself that I was doing the right thing because maybe what God wanted for me wasn't what I had planned. Maybe He wanted me to give up my will for His. Well… I certainly don't think that way now.

It's important that we know, and that we teach our children to know, that God has placed certain desires in our hearts and that when we are walking in His will, we can trust those desires. I have no doubt today, that the desires of my heart are exactly what God intends for me to have in His perfect timing (Psalm 37:4). However, because of the amazing journey I have had, I have no regrets. But I must admit; it was a horrible detour to go through in order to get to the place I am today.

You see, all I focused on was God's favor in his life. Doors just seemed to open for him where ever he went. I was amazed and I wanted to be around that. It's just too bad I didn't realize that God's favor was something that I could have for myself too (Psalm 5:12/Proverbs 12:2). But it is what it is and I don't think there is anything that could explain why I did what I did and yet I could find a thousand possibilities but no real answers.

Had my eyes been open to other things, I might have learned that this man I was dating, and was later married to, was actually battling some very serious demons; alcohol, drugs, sex, you name it. How then was he ministering? I don't know but I can imagine he was very torn apart inside as he did. I believe when he was seeking God he was very genuine and God used him to minister to others and bring them to salvation, not for his benefit but for theirs. God is looking for vessels who are available. God can use anyone to reach the lost. At times we are appalled at the men we see used in ministry. We sit back and judge them for all their shortcomings. We call them hypocrites for living a life that does not reflect the Word they are preaching. And yet we are so comfortable in our own salvation that we sit in our cozy pews and do nothing but watch. Perhaps if we ourselves were upright and standing ready for action, we would have fewer mixed messages or "double agents" out there. He reminded me of the poem of the little girl (or boy, as I will use in this case) who had a little curl right in the middle of his forehead and when he was good he was very, very good but when he was bad, he was horrid.

And thus is life with a double agent. When things were good "they were very, very good". We were missionaries in Costa Rica for about 6 months and pastored a Spanish church in Southern California. The ministry aspect was incredible. It was amazing to see the hand of

God move in so many ways and in so many lives. I loved ministering to the women and the children. It is amazing how much love a heart can hold when you begin to pray for others. You become a tight-knit family. The ministry was a gift I was honored to be a part of. But that's pretty much where the good times ended. Home life felt more like a curse than a blessing. I mean, we had our moments but that's all they were… moments. I had a great time in ministry and learned a lot; the good, the bad and the ugly. But it was a desperate spirit in me that cried out to God for a rescue. Something was wrong and I didn't know what. I was battling an invisible enemy in the form of a pastor-gone-bad. I felt like I was living with Dr. Jekyll and Mr. Hyde. I kept praying for a change in him but what I got... was a change in me.

"And when they were bad, they were horrid". He was controlling and manipulative, abusive physically, emotionally and financially. I was a prisoner in my own home, walking on egg shells with each tick of the clock. I awoke each morning with a question in my head… will this be a good day or a bad day? I could usually tell within the first five minutes and it usually was not the answer I was hoping for.

I wasn't allowed to be in any other room unless all the children were with me.   It was stifling. I would get countless phone calls at work from him checking up on me and threatening me not to be a minute late. And yet when I would get home, I can remember standing just outside the door and telling myself, "I could leave. I don't have to open that door. I can leave and never come back." But then I would hear the beautiful little voices from inside and I knew I could never leave my children behind. I had to get in there quickly... and so I did.

There were times while we were driving, that I would be the recipient of colorful bruises on my thighs or arms because some guy, whom I didn't even notice, would look over at me (or more accurately, he would glance to the right or left to take in his surroundings as any safe driver would do). We even got into a car accident once when he purposely slammed our car into the vehicle of a male classmate who said "hi" to me in the parking lot. There were other events I do not remember but others have retold to me. Sometimes I still can't remember them even after they have been told to me. I can picture them at that point, but that's about as close to a memory as I can stir up - and I don't know if its a memory or just me trying to picture what their words are illustrating. I lost a lot of memories of my married years so there is so much that I cannot explain.

The hardest part of losing those memories was realizing that I had lost them. Think about it, if you don't have memories of something, you don't know they ever existed. So how could you know something was lost? A friend of mine was told by another friend of something he witnessed. It was years later when they asked me how I made it through such an attack that I even remembered it happened but this is one of those memories that definitely came flooding back...

I had gone into the kitchen to get a towel to wipe up a spill. Unfortunately, I used a rag that was intended to clean dry spills on this wet spill. Before I knew it, our dinner guest was left at the table and I was on the ground in a ball trying to protect my unborn baby (I was seven months pregnant at the time) from the onslaught of kicks I was receiving from my husband. I remember our guest (my husband's friend) was yelling for him to stop, granting a long enough distraction for me to drag my hurt body to the bedroom. Beyond that, I do not remember. I don't know how I made it through that. I don't know when it was blocked out; if the memory was lost years later, days later, or even moments later. And for the life of me, I can't imagine how I could stay with someone who could do that!

There is no wonder I lost that memory. How could I even face another day if I had? There were plenty of those moments though, and unfortunately, some of them were brought back to mind not only by friends and family members but also through my children's retelling of the events. So when was enough, enough? When would it all come to an end?

The man that I had looked to as a Godly example was the exact opposite (de ja vu). Yet I saw God work through him even in the worst of times. What a horrible position to be in as a wife. What do you do? You cry out to God. You believe that God has great plans in store and that is why the enemy is attacking so hard. You pray for change. You see none. You cry out again. You cannot imagine living through another day. You hope for death. And then you hope no more. Then you exchange faith for negotiation on a bathroom floor.

At least, that's what I did…

-3-
The Negotiating Room

Before I take you to the negotiating room, there is one thing I need to make clear. I had already tried to accomplish my goals in my own ways and on my own terms. When people come to the place of negotiation, it is usually because they were unable to come to a resolution on their own, so having exhausted all other avenues; they must come to a place of compromise instead.

One of the most common questions that arise when people discover that someone is in an abusive relationship is "why don't they just leave?' Well, there are many reasons to leave, all of them obvious. But the reasons they stay are far more complicated. I cannot explain why I stayed as long as I did nor why I left when I did because things are not always so cut and dry. So instead, I will share a bit of the roller coaster ride with you and the thought process behind it.
I was living with my husband for less than half of our marriage. We were separated three times. Each time, with exception to the third, I allowed him back in our home. Don't ask why now, just read on and I'll try my best to let you in. Before our first separation, I remember my main battle being my belief in my husband and his potential (a dangerous word; it's only a good thing when it is in the process of being actualized). I was ever the encouraging wife, always pushing him to not let failure keep him from pursuing his ministry; God had bigger plans for him and it was natural that

21

the enemy would try to keep him from accomplishing them. I
was so set on my role as the encourager (which was a
smooth transition to enabler) that I failed to accept the reality
of what was before me. I even hid the abuse so expertly on
the chance that it would end. I would not want to tarnish his
reputation. If I did, he would never return to the ministry and
the outcome of that would mean I would be left with "Mr.
Hyde" on a full time basis. No thanks! I preferred to hope
that the good Dr. Jekyll would one day return.

On the bad days when I would feel hopelessness
sinking in, I would begin to paint a mental picture. I would try
to imagine our family ten years down the road gathered
around a Christmas tree, enjoying our family time. I have no
idea where I got that imagery or why it always had to be
Christmas. I probably just heard it somewhere and decided
it was worth a shot to pull me through the tough times. In
any case, I would then ask myself if I was willing to give up
that future (that was real only in my mind) because I wasn't
strong enough to endure the present hard times. This
became a vital picture because as the years continued on, I
could no longer paint it, not even in my imagination. It was
laughable in the face of the reality around me. So although,
it kept me in an unsafe place for a time, it also allowed me to
break free in the future.

I also battled with my own personal and religious
views. Marriage was forever. I could will myself to endure it
no matter how awful it got just to keep my promise. It wasn't
the vow that I made to my husband that concerned me, but
rather the vow that I made to God. I couldn't bring myself to
break that. It was inconceivable. No, I could make it
through this. I would learn to avoid the land mines and live
in a loveless marriage if that was the cost. Why not? I made
my bed and now I would have to lay in it.

It wasn't until that night in the negotiating room, however, that I realized that God had a different plan. I could not begin to imagine what it was but I knew that if I "stayed in my bed" it would not be to lay in it, but rather it would be to die in it! But before I explain what happened that night, I will take you through the first and second separations and the God-lessons I learned…

Our first separation came just two or three days after the birth of our third child. My husband would come and go with a particular friend of his. They would often come back late and his friend would sleep over. I didn't trust him and never felt comfortable with him around my girls. After we returned home from the hospital with the new baby, to my detriment, his friend was also there. My husband was always a jealous man and suspicious on top of that. He would get angry at me if his friend, who I wished would just disappear from our home, would so much as carry on a conversation with me. I finally told him that he needed to choose; he either tells his friend to leave our home or he could go with him... so, he left.

He was gone for the next eight months. He would come around once in a while and play "proud papa" but he never stayed long. However, I was determined that God wasn't done with our marriage so I began what I call my mission to pray him back. This is important because the next time it would happen; there would be a different sentiment behind my mission. Sometimes God's yes's are not necessarily His best for you, as I will soon explain (remember King Saul? 1 Samuel 8-12).

The second time we separated, I was the one who left. That is when the physical abuse became a constant as opposed to a rare occurrence. I had a good job and our home was actually included as part of the compensation.

Because we worked together, I felt trapped. I thought if I left, I would lose my job as well. Later, I was to find out that wasn't the case, but I was rash and acted quickly, never giving my boss a chance to work things out on his end. What was the rush? I had obviously had plenty of experience on waiting things out. But this time was different. I had just found out that I was pregnant. I didn't tell him for a couple of weeks after finding out. For the first time ever, I cried over the thought of having a child. It wasn't the child that I was rejecting but rather bringing another child into this abusive environment. It was too much for me. I told him the news that I was expecting and how I felt about it. I also told him that I was quitting my job and leaving so he would be wise to start packing his stuff as well. He thought I was bluffing, never for once believing I would leave my cushy job and home, let alone him. So I picked up the receiver and dialed my boss…

It wasn't until my son was born that I began to rethink my situation. Was it really fair to rob my son and daughters of a family, especially when they would need a father? It had been a long time, and I thought perhaps my husband had changed. I remembered hearing God speak to my heart one day. It was so clear. I had been telling Him, "I prayed him back once before, I'll just do it again." I wasn't actually expecting a response. It was more of a statement than a question. But I remember God's answer because it felt more like a warning than anything else, "Only because you asked." It left me with a feeling of foreboding and I knew I was in the wrong but still it sounded like a yes to me. It was as if God, in His Father-to-child tone of voice, was telling me, "This is not the plan I have for you, but since you are being so stubborn, I am going to give you exactly what you asked for. You can learn the hard way." And so I did. There were times when I wondered why God didn't come to my rescue sooner. But when I go back and connect the dots, the correct question would be; why didn't I let Him?

So it was some months later when I found myself in yet another new home but in the same old story. It was a rough night, my oldest daughter (4 years old) had suffered a bloody nose and her sister (3 years old) just about had the spirit slapped out of her for interrupting a movie her father was watching. Needless to say, I was not going to merely stand by and watch, so I placed myself between them and absorbed what was left of his onslaught before he returned to his movie as though nothing had happened. It was then that I hired a babysitter to watch my children while I was at work (even though their father was home). We didn't need the additional cost but I could no longer trust him to be home alone with the kids.

It was a few days later when I found myself in the kitchen washing dishes, after the family had fallen asleep, that I came to grips with a thought that truly frightened me. I was holding the cutting knife I used to cut the chicken for dinner. I was getting flash backs to another time when that same knife was held against my throat. My husband and I had both been in the kitchen in what I had thought was a peaceful time. Before I knew what happened, he was in front of me with the knife pressed against my throat. I was more in shock than frightened. It was completely unexpected as it had been a calm evening.

Where was this coming from? He had this crazed look in his eye (it was a forced look as if he was just trying to play the part of psycho to scare me) and he was saying things like, "I could do it, you know. You don't think I will, do you? How could you be so sure? I don't even know. All it takes is one second and then I couldn't take the moment back, even if I wanted to." He just held the knife there against my throat (not pressing hard but not removing it either) as my mind went racing in all sorts of directions, still trying to make sense of it all.

I thought of ways I could get away but then I thought of how this could be my way for it all to be finally over. That thought didn't last too long though as my thoughts shifted to how the children needed me. I thought of God and wondered if this was really all my life would come to – and I believed it was not. I knew I had more to do, yet in that moment I wasn't quite sure how I would ever accomplish it. And that's when it all stopped. He laughed and turned back to the dinner we were cooking, asking me to pass him one of the dishes, as if it were all a passing joke. That was the end of the flashback but given the events of the day, I came to a startling realization; if I didn't get out soon, one of us would end up dead and I wasn't so sure it would be me.

It was that night when the children were sleeping and I was in the bathroom, running the water to wash my face, that my thoughts began to run wild. I was desperate to end it all – this thing called life. I knew I didn't have it in me to leave but I was more than ready to let him go. I still hadn't come to terms with the idea that leaving would be acceptable in the eyes of God. But I simply couldn't go on with the ways things were. I had hoped and prayed for far too long that my husband would change and we could have peace in our marriage. But things only got worse. Surely God was turning a deaf ear on my prayers. Surely He didn't care. If He did, He would have stepped in by now. At this time, I still had no clue what my husband was involved in (drugs, alcohol, women, etc.). All I was aware of was what I saw. I was too naïve to know any better. I didn't know anything about those worlds so I missed all of the clues that I probably would have noticed if I wasn't so sheltered.

I knew this man who was in ministry was seriously mistreating his wife and family and that was more than enough to know something was not right in God's eyes. I knew his actions were a manifestation of something bigger but I didn't know what. So that night in the bathroom, now turned negotiating room, I laid it all out before God.

I left the water running and turned it on even higher. I am not sure why but I was transfixed by its power. Maybe the sound if it rushing would drown out my own desperate thoughts. Maybe I wanted the sound to mask my cries. I don't know what it was but it brought me some sense of sanity. I thought of ending my life there at the bathroom sink, to find freedom in the sound of that rushing water. I ran through the various ways I could accomplish the task. But before I could decide, there was a voice in my mind trying desperately to be heard and in a barely audible voice were the words that stopped me in my tracks; *"But that wouldn't be me."* Me… Me? Who was this "me" anyway? Who had I become? I remember the young woman I was growing up and in high school but that person was gone, or so I thought. I had become an empty shell of a person with no opinions and no…dare I say it? No hope.

But I was wrong. Deep inside I was still that person, which is why the abuse had never been accepted. I never once thought I deserved it, as so many victims are depicted to believe and I never once thought it was my fault. But still, the longer I stayed, the more lost I became. But that voice was still there, no matter how faint. And that night it was heard as if it was shouting from the rooftops. "But that wouldn't be me!" I wasn't a quitter and I certainly wouldn't run away from my children. No, I couldn't do that but I also couldn't continue on. It was time to negotiate before it was too late. I was also wrong about the hope. I had to have at least one small sliver left or I couldn't have even started the conversation with God I was about to initiate. I pressed up against the wall and sank to the floor. And that's when the negotiations began...

It started out something like this; "Okay God, first things first, I don't know what my husband is up to. But I know there is something very wrong going on here. I am here to support my husband because it is what YOU require of me, as his wife. But I beg You, Lord, please do not hold me accountable for whatever it is he is doing." That was something that weighed very heavily on my heart, especially as the wife of a pastor with so much accountability, and I needed to get that out in the open. But I wasn't finished there. No, that's when I began to make demands on the Creator of the Universe, God Almighty. And as horribly out of line as I was, He still listened! Sometimes it doesn't matter what we say, even when we are so off base. What is important is that we open up that line of communication. God is bigger than all of our tantrums and He has a way of bringing us back into line, reminding us of both our place and His. You would be amazed how many of our hurtful monologues can turn into healing dialogues with God. Remember, He is a relational God and He will not hesitate to get involved in your life but first, you need to open up and invite Him in.

Here were the terms of my negotiation; I would not end my life for the period of two years. After that, God would have had to change my life completely or I would take it into my own hands.   I didn't want just any change; I was ready for God to turn it completely upside down, if necessary. I also prayed that if it was His will that I be free from this marriage then He would have to make it so that my husband was the one to leave. And to top it off, it would be done in a peaceful manner, so that I would know it was His hand and not that of the enemy.

That was all there was to it. Apparently I thought I had some leverage in which I could use to negotiate with God. That's pretty absurd when you consider that all that I am and have is in Him and through Him. But He was well aware that his wayward daughter was speaking out of hurt and desperation. And I suppose He didn't hold it against me because what happened next was exactly what I asked for.

I don't have a good grasp on timing due to the blocked memories, but I do know that it was during a time that his sister had moved in with us, that he went downstairs with a bag of laundry, never to return again. I didn't even know he had left for good. I thought he had just gone on another one of his adventures; the ones where he wouldn't come back until late at night or the next day.

But my children began to talk about something he had told them before he left. He let them know that he would be leaving and that they shouldn't be sad because they would see him one day in heaven. He was trying to prepare them for his departure and he must have done a good job because they never once shed a tear for him. But more than that, I believe it was God who put a hedge of protection around them, even to this day, to keep their hearts safe and whole. But there we were, after so many fights over nothing at all, and suddenly I was free without so much as a raised voice or a threatening gesture. My prayers had been answered.

But I had much more to deal with than his departure. I had to move soon, or by law, he could return to his home within 6 months (or so I was told by the officers who came to our home on occasion). I lost more than the obvious when he left. I lost my ministry, my church, my job, my house, a few friends and eventually my car. But you know what? I got it all back, everything new, everything better… and all of it within two years. And true to form, spoiled child of God that I am, I didn't even notice it happening until the two years were up!

-4-
Following the Leader

The transition period was a little difficult to go through. My husband didn't only leave his family but the ministry as well. I remember the first service after he left. It was actually the same evening. My sister-in-law and I pulled together to make it through the service. She played the guitar for praise and worship and I gave my first sermon in Spanish. After the service we had a meeting with the elders of the church and decided that the best thing would be to find them a local church. So we sought out a well-respected pastor for them. But before they had the chance to attend the new church, my husband returned (not home, but to the church).

My sister-in-law and I spoke to them and let them know that if he returned, we could not stay with them. Although we knew it was ill advised for them to accept him as a leader, we were sure to remind them that whatever he may do, he is only a man. Their acceptance of him spoke volumes to their forgiving heart and that was a beautiful gesture. But it was important for them to know how to separate the sins of man from the love of God, not just in this instance but for life in general. They remained with him for a short time after that. However, it wasn't very long before he ended up leaving again. But thank God they had grown enough spiritually to continue to move forward. From what I hear, they are all doing well and are in wonderful churches.

But still, leaving the ministry left me with a new dilemma: I no longer had a church to attend and the weekend was fast approaching.

It was imperative to me that we find a place to attend that Sunday. The children had too much change in their lives. I needed them to know that God was something that would always be a constant. Now, I know that God is not in a building but as young children there is a definite association there that they were able to understand. My closest friend at the time invited me to go to church with her. After all the stress we were going through as a family, it was nice to look forward to something. She mentioned another local church that I might be interested in but we were already excited about going together. So that weekend we went together to her church.

As we were walking out after service, I remember thinking to myself how unfair life was. I was filling my mind with thoughts of self-pity. As we were walking to the car I heard God speak to me, once again in that Father-like voice. Only this time, it was not to a stubborn child but to a spoiled one. And this is what I heard "How dare you…?" The words came slowly and clearly and I began to cringe in anticipation of some daunting message from that familiar Voice. However, as it continued, I was to learn that it was a much gentler message than I had anticipated. "How dare you think such thoughts? Are you the one suffering here? You have your children with you. You are not on the street looking for a place to stay, unsure of where your next meal will come from, alone and without family. No… I am holding you in the nook of my arms. I am cooing you as a parent does to comfort a tearful infant. How dare you feel sorry for yourself… when you have Me?"

I was so overwhelmed by those words that the tears began to spill over as I walked toward the car. My friend was puzzled so I explained to her what I heard. Instead of looking at me like I was crazy, making things up in my head, she just nodded in a knowing fashion. She told me there was something she had to share with me. She told me that as much as she loves the idea of our families going to church together, she couldn't shake the conviction that she was to send me elsewhere. It was then that she told me once again of the church nearby named Palm View. She said she had only been to the Spanish ministry but that it was a very friendly church and she felt like God wouldn't let her rest until she told me to check it out. So I made a phone call and got the schedule for the next week's service. I'd never actually gone to a church on my own. I was always taken somewhere by someone I knew. But if God was calling me in that direction then it is the way I would go. As long as He showed up, I was guaranteed to know the most important person there.

I remember the first time I set foot at Palm View. I remember the joy and freedom I felt in the midst of that congregation. It was such a complete contrast from the brokenness I felt inside. But there I was, in the midst of all that joy and I knew in my heart that it was okay to let it all sink in. I didn't have to be skeptical of it or unsure of whether I should reach out for that joy only to have it slip through my grasp again. There was something different this time. I had been set free and through a puzzling set of circumstances I found myself led to this church, to this moment, where the presence, joy and freedom of the Lord were so evident. It was a new beginning for me.

Although my hope had always been in the Lord, my life to that point had never seen so much joy and celebration. It was a heavily burdened life but I trudged through it with the strength that only the Lord could bring. Being there in that moment was overwhelming. It was like a child finding out that fairytales were real, that every good thing they ever believed in truly did exist. And the tears poured and poured. I could not stop the flow. It was as if God was cleansing me from the inside out of all the hurt that I had been carrying inside for so long. And from the outside I may have looked like a soul in utter devastation but that was the furthest thing from the truth. I had found an abundance of hope. I felt released from the prison that no one even knew I was in. The charade was up, game over. I could finally just "*be*".

Although that morning may have been spent in tears, by the time I had returned for the second service, I had already crossed over to that place of joy. I could never have imagined such a drastic change and in so very little time. But it was that day, just seven years ago, that changed how I would live the rest of my life. I even remember the prayer requests that evening. As Pastor Joseph took those requests, Sister Esther (my lighthouse) said that we needed "to pray for that young lady over there because she has a beautiful voice." To my astonishment she was pointing to me, half way across the sanctuary. It seemed like such an odd reason to pray for a person that I couldn't help but smile as a slight chuckle escaped. Of course she had no idea what those words meant to me. But after having a ministry ripped away, I felt so lost. Ministry was the one thing I knew I wanted for my life. It was the only thing I was sure of. When it was ripped away I felt as though I was nobody in the eyes of God. However, the message I heard was different from the words that were spoken. What I heard was a reminder from God letting me know that no matter what size the crowd I was in, He would still see me. I would never be lost to Him.

It was ironic though that she chose to mention my voice because singing was the one thing I would be asked to stop doing as I did my chores around the house. The girls and I would always fill the house with praise and worship but when my husband would be home, I was ordered to stop because he couldn't stand the sound of it (not praise and worship – just me). Even more ironic was the fact that God would use that very thing, my voice, to open new doors of ministry in ways I never dreamed to imagine. But God brought me to a place where I would discover my spiritual gifts and would be able to explore them and grow in them with freedom. I thank God for my church family and I thank God for giving me a voice, not only musically, but a voice to proclaim His Word, to speak of the great things He has done and to give Him the glory He so deserves.

Pastor Joseph and his wife, Doreen soon became my spiritual parents. They took me in as a daughter and encouraged me along the road to recovery. Encouragement is something that we often take for granted, but it has a powerful way of bringing life to a person. I got involved in just about everything I could; I worked in the nursery, children's church, taught Sunday school and sang on the worship team. I was like a sponge trying to soak up as much as I could and give back as much as I could release. But it never felt like I had found my place. These were all areas that I was able to contribute in but there was something else… I wouldn't figure out what that something else was until years later. I am still trying to piece it together but I have a much clearer idea. But what I did stumble on was fascinating.

I began to write songs. I am not sure that is a fair statement because it was more like I was given songs to pen. I would get a mental image, then the words would come and the melody was already with it. There was nothing really creative about it. It felt almost like cheating. It was definitely a gift, in the truest sense of the word. Only I came upon a stumbling block; I had the words and melody in my head but I had no way of translating that into music (unless you count humming). At first my sister-in-law would help compose the songs but that soon became frustrating. I loved working with her to piece things together but we were both single moms and our "quiet" times were far and few between. So I decided to pick up the guitar and teach myself with a few books and a whole lot of prayer; *teach my hands to war and my fingers to fight (Psalm 144:1)*. Soon I was both writing and composing. It's amazing what God can do with even the smallest steps you take in the direction He leads. That wasn't the first time I would take a step in God's direction only to find myself swept away on an amazing new journey, and it certainly wouldn't be the last.

One of the most amazing journey's I have been on came a couple of years after I began attending Palm View; I began to break away from the children's ministry and started working as a youth counselor. It was on a trip to Magic Mountain that I learned that one of the young girls wanted to stop coming to church. She didn't feel she fit in and as we continued to talk, her brother joined us and I also learned that neither one of them knew how to pray. I began to ask them more questions and soon I realized their need for discipleship. I told them if she would agree to stay a little while longer, I would commit to visiting them and having bible studies at their house. They both agreed and a few weeks later we started what we thought would be a small intimate study time.

When I got to their house, I was pleased to see that their younger sister also decided to join us. We sat at the kitchen table and began our study. Their uncle had been visiting and at the end of the study he asked if he could bring his grandson the following week. Who was I to say no? I was thrilled that I went from having two to four students in just one week. What a blessing! But things didn't turn out as planned. Summer had begun and my children were out of school. I had nowhere to take them but with me. As I realized that, I began to think this study idea might not work out after all. The family had a small place and with my four kids plus the four youth I was teaching, it would be too much for me (and the house). But then I met a woman who would come to our rescue.

I dropped by the house to deliver a bible that I had bought for one of the youth when I saw their neighbor from across the street. I was introduced to her once and although I could hardly say that I knew her, I did know who she was and that she was close to the family. So I walked across the street to ask her if she could deliver the bible for me. That's when I began to speak from a will that was not my own. There were words coming out of my mouth that I could not stop and I couldn't believe what I was saying. I spoke with a boldness I cannot explain. And despite that voice in my head that kept saying, "You don't even know this woman," I found myself telling her about the bible study dilemma and I mentioned how I noticed that she had a large backyard… (I think she knew what direction I was going by now) so I dropped the proverbial bomb and asked her if we could have the study at her house and by some miracle of God… she agreed. She didn't just agree, she was excited and said that her husband knew some of the neighborhood kids and that she would let them know about it too. That was fine by me, with the additional space, what's a couple more?

When I showed up on Thursday I was amazed to find that there were about 12 kids there. I had no idea she meant all the neighborhood kids, at least that's what it seemed like. Her husband peeked out back and informed me that a lot of kids couldn't come but that they would be there the following week. And that study grew faster than I could have imagined. The next week there were 20 kids, then 25 and so on. Soon we had about 35-40 kids coming to study from grades K-12. And with the growth came the workers. We ended up with four teachers and two hostesses. We would have praise and worship all together and then split up into the older and younger groups. The smaller children even had a craft time. We had pizza, drinks and baked goods. It was amazing how everyone came together and donated their time, talents, money and hearts. And to think it all started because one child was about to leave the youth group.

Every last one of us makes a difference, in our good times and in our troubled times. Those of us who reach out in our troubled times shine a light on a need that Christ wants to fill. Those of us who have come out of troubled times have a heart that relates and can bring a story of hope to those currently going through difficult times. And when we find ourselves in a good place, it is important for us to reach out to others so we can help them find their way as well. It is so important that we plug into ministry because not only does it bless others but it blesses us as well. On my own, I would have been very limited but as a team, we were able to accomplish something bigger than ourselves.

Most of those children did not go to church at all. Some came from very tough homes. I remember one day we witnessed a young boy's mother get taken away by the police. Their father was already in custody. Both were facing serious charges and we were later told that neither of them would be returning soon. We stood there watching the horrible scene unfold, not knowing what to do or how to help this young boy out. But then he helped us. He ran over to his grandmother and said, "Jesus will bring her back. I know

He will…" His grandmother just shook her head and looked down at him, when he finished his sentence, "because He loves me." My faith was challenged that night. What happens when they don't come back? Oh, how I asked God to help me in my unbelief (Mark 9:24)! This child needed more from our prayers than just going through the motions. A couple of weeks later (maybe less), we learned that his mother, who was facing some serious time away, was now home. My faith grew immeasurably that day and I have a 5 year old to thank for it.

Unfortunately, there are roadblocks on our journeys. And this one ended after about 8 months. It crushed my heart to say goodbye but I know that we made a difference in a lot of lives. We even had young leaders rise up and start bible studies at their schools. I remember one of them would always take my lesson plans every week and would even ask for any notes I had scribbled down anywhere. But soon he and his friend were creating lesson plans of their own.

I continue to pray for those kids even today. I pray that great things would come from their lives and that they would always walk closely with the Lord. I consider it an amazing honor and privilege to have had any part of that experience at all. If the opportunity should present itself to pour the love of Christ into a young child's life, I pray that you take it. It will do more than change their life; it will change yours.

-5-

No U-Turns Allowed

The years after the divorce were not all fun and sunshine. There were definitely a lot of obstacles on the course. There were times they seemed so daunting that I just wanted to turn around and head back in the other direction. But there was something within me that pushed me forward, driven with the need to see what lay at the end of the course. There may have been hurdles but they only came as I moved further along the course. So I just kept reminding myself that every time those obstacles came they were only markers representing all the progress and ground I had covered. And when I kept focused on that mental picture, there just didn't seem to be any sense in going back.

Some of the obstacles came through years of financial struggle (which most, if not all, people can relate to); losing homes, vehicles, childcare, jobs, etc. Times were tough enough when we were barely making ends meet but to struggle only to lose something every time I came up for air was enough to threaten my sanity. But it also tempted me to doubt God and His provisions. No, I didn't ever doubt that God was my source but the opportunity sure did present itself in times like those and I was sure getting weary of His creative ways (if you know what I mean). We always had what we needed, we just never knew where it was coming from until it showed up and always just in the nick of time. Sometimes I wished we could have had things the boring

40

way but God chose to do it His way instead (which is always the best way). I needed to know He was there for me and it was the perfect way to teach my kids that they had a Father in heaven that would always provide for them and Who would never leave them nor forsake them (Hebrews 13:5b). Of course, I could have taught them that through scriptures alone but living the Word helps them to own the promises written. And to this day when things just seem to fall in place, they are able to recognize God's hand in every detail.

Other obstacles threatened the new friendships that had blossomed; some were tested, some were strained and others would fade as people moved away. Each friendship was precious and the trials brought a lot of heartache because I held them all so dear. But there was growth that needed to take place in each of us and each situation served its purpose. I learned that forgiveness doesn't always mean acceptance. I learned that even the closest people will disappoint you. I also learned that sometimes the people who we think love us the most, do so under their own conditions (whether intentionally or not) and when those conditions are not met, you are quickly discarded. But that is a reflection of the individual and *not you*. It's important to discern the difference so you don't put yourself in a position that could potentially destroy you (pain, anger, bitterness, resentment, and hurt or an unforgiving heart).

I learned that rejection doesn't always mean you are not good enough, sometimes it is the other person who is not good enough and other times it has nothing to do with the people involved at all but rather it was just the situation that was not good enough; that God just has something different planned, something better. We can do some pretty ridiculous things when we don't comprehend these things – we end up holding onto things and people that we know are not good for us in order to prove a point we don't even understand to an audience we can't identify and we end up making a bigger mess of our lives than we began with. I call this behavior "holding onto what we don't want for reasons we don't understand." I also learned that you can't always lean on the strong friends around you; there comes a time when you have to stand on your own – you'll have no doubt when that moment comes because you'll be dialing the phone and knocking on doors but no one will answer. Eventually, you'll find yourself at a park or in some shopping area parked in your car, alone and …finally… crying out to God. And as much as you love these friendships, there comes a time when you might have to let some of them go. I had a lot to learn in those years and those lessons came with a lot of tears and heartache but they were worth every bit of it.

I was no longer an empty shell of a person. I was rediscovering who I was along the way. I don't mean that in the grand scheme of things. I mean I began to discover the very basic things about me; my talents, my love for music, art, writing, sports, stars and waterfalls. I was able to identify that my favorite color was blue, a question I could not answer for many years and for the life of me, I never knew why. I had lost all knowledge of the things that made me unique. I always went with the flow, so as not to invite conflict, and as a result I soon had no opinions and knew very little about what I wanted or liked.

But through all those friendships, even the ones that did not endure and the ones that perhaps endured a bit too long, I rediscovered myself. In my heart of hearts, I consider them all the dearest of friends and I will hold them there for as long as I live. They know who they are, of that I have no doubt. If they should ever read these words, I would have them know how grateful I am to have had them in my life and how very much I love them. I think that's important. There are many times that great friendships end and leave behind a bitter taste but that's not how friendships should be. It only hurts so much because we care so deeply. How can we be so quick to forget that?

Some friendships end because people move away or move on with their lives and the ones who stay behind can sometimes resent that and they feel abandoned. We need to change our perspectives and start valuing the gifts we were given. Just because a relationship has ended, that does not mean you have to lose a friend. You toss the bad, keep the good and carry them in your heart. They become a part of you. There are those that will be by your side for the long run. Praise God for them . But for those that leave, honor the times you shared together and cherish that season. I will close this chapter with a poem I wrote about friendship. It seems only fitting since it would serve as a tribute to those who inspired it.

In life, we will go through the most amazing journeys. But that is not to say they will not be sprinkled with heartaches. But if we try to see them through God's perspective, we will know that even they have their place. As we continue to put our trust in God, we will begin to see His will unfold as we gain peace and more understanding of how He is working in our lives. We can never truly go back... and why would we want to? There are just some U-turns we should never take. But we can always go forward (Joshua 1:9).

A Friend Worth Keeping

There are friends that come and friends that go
But a friend that stays, I'll have you know
... is a friend worth keeping.

A friend that loves you through the pain,
One who forgives with nothing to gain
... is a friend worth keeping.

A friend that knows when to let go
For just a season so you can grow
... is a friend worth keeping.

A friend who is always there for you
To push you forward and pray you through
... is a friend worth keeping.

A friend who's there to lift your head
Despite the tears you've made them shed
... is a friend worth keeping.
They give from their heart in all that they do
They encourage and believe in you.
If a certain friend comes to your heart
I pray your paths may never part.

But if they do, I hope and pray
That God would bring them back one day.
And when He does, you hang on tight
And love them back with all your might!

-6-

Identity Crisis – You Complete Me

During a Sunday morning service, our church had a special group of young adults come to give their testimonies. All of them were powerful testimonies but one of them really struck a chord with me. A young lady was talking about her journey to finding her identity. I had never quite thought of it the way she put it. I think all of us are aware of our seemingly endless search for our ever elusive identity and we struggle so hard to find it.

This young lady though, saw it in a completely different perspective, and perhaps a more accurate one. You see, we spend so much of our time trying to figure out who we are but in reality we probably have too many identities and need to do some down-sizing. This young lady said it wasn't finding her identity that was hard – the hard part was keeping track of all of them and hoping that their paths never collided (which they eventually did). She said she was brought to a point where she had to make a decision on what she wanted her identity to be, so she chose the church. She then went on to say that it was the wrong choice because we are supposed to "be" the church, not find our identity in it. Our identity needs to be in Christ.

It was a pretty powerful testimony and I think so many of us can relate, especially our younger generation who are struggling with finding their way out of childhood and into

45

adulthood. As we grow we find ourselves falling into many different roles; we are one person at home, one person at school, one person with friends, and yet another at church and so on. It's not that we are trying to live separate lives and we are certainly not trying to live a lie. We simply have so many aspects to our identity and some are more comfortably expressed in some situations than they are in others. The caution comes in making sure that we never contradict the *essence* of who we are. We shouldn't be afraid to have all those identities collide. Our goal however, is to find a place where all those attributes find harmony and we can be "ourselves" wherever we are . I think it's when we come to that point that we begin to say, "I finally found myself."

For most people, a general sense of who you are develops at a young age and becomes more defined with the passing years. But sometimes we find ourselves in situations where we just feel "lost". I don't know why this happens. Each person who experiences this finds themselves there through different catalysts. For some, the loss of a loved one has them questioning who they are and what their role is in life. For example when a woman loses her husband to death she is no longer in the role of "wife" and has to redefine herself in her mind. She is the same person but she feels lost. The same thing happens when parents lose their children and vice versa, when a hard working employee or businessman becomes disabled and can no longer work, and when people experience life altering accidents or traumatic events.

As for me, I don't know exactly when I "lost myself". I once believed it was when I began dating and eventually married my ex-husband. I had become such a peacekeeper that I would do, say and think anything I had to in order to prevent a violent outbreak. I was always walking on eggshells and pretty soon it became second nature and most of the time I wasn't even aware I was doing it. It wasn't until after my final separation from my ex that I began to realize I had no opinion for myself. Without anyone there to force their opinion on me, I didn't know what to think. I couldn't make the simplest of decisions because I didn't know what I wanted. I didn't know what kind of food I liked, what hobbies I liked or what my favorite color was. It was then that I realized I was lost. Once upon a time I knew all of those answers and I was determined to learn them again.

But as I said, I "thought" that was when I lost myself. But I think the truth is I lost myself years before that when I was a child learning to cope with abuse. From the moment abuse occurs and a child is left to determine their response to it, they begin to lose themselves. Their actions then begin to put others first: Who do I tell? Who will get hurt? Should I just stay quiet? How do I know what the right thing to do is? And who determines what is right? You feel like any action or lack of action that you take is wrong so you begin to take the one that hurts the least amount of people.

At least that's what I told myself I was doing. From then on it was always about pleasing people. I had to be the best at everything (and I mean "had" to). If I even thought I was second best at anything it would tear me apart. So I grew up an overachiever, which as a result helped me to refine many of my skills and talents. But as strong and confident as I was in my abilities, I still found myself in a relationship that would suck the life out of me and leave me an empty shell of a person. To this day I kept saying I didn't know how that could happen to such a strong and confident person. But now I realize that my strength and confidence were not in myself, but rather in the perception of me that I created for the approval of others.

It wasn't until I sat down with my daughter one day and had one of those conversations about "staying true to your self" that I realized the truth in the above statement. She had gotten herself into some trouble. It was minor trouble but it was the first time she had made a decision that seemed so out of character for her. She had told me she didn't want to do it but she wanted her friend to like her so she would keep coming to church with her. So we talked about God drawing the people to Him and that she shouldn't worry about that part, since God's got it covered. But then we discussed how she shouldn't worry about what others thought of her, so long as she was true to herself. Then her eyes filled with tears and I realized what the problem was so I told her, "I know… you don't even know who that is." She shook her head and the tears poured.

She too is an overachiever, always trying to be the best at all that she can. And there is no question about her search for approval. I have very high standards for my kids and I let them know it. But I don't stress when they fall short and I tell them not to stress either. I ask them if they did their best and if they did then they can be proud (I think that is a high enough standard for anyone in anything). And that seems to work with academics but character issues are a bit harder. My little mini-me is quite the follower. I, on the other hand, am more of a leader. But I forget that for most of my life, I was that follower too. Not so much in moral issues but in my basic decision making. It was a definite process for me. Only, my daughter has the benefit of picking my brain.

I talked to her about what my struggles were in finding myself, hoping to help her on her journey. Gratefully, she said she related to everything I was sharing with her (sometimes I think I am going to sound like I am making no sense because "moms don't understand"). Then my mom came in the room and we started speaking into my daughter's life, the things that we saw in her; recognizing her strengths, weaknesses, passions, and personality traits. She soaked it all in and I immediately began to see a transformation in how she held herself. It reminded me of how it was that very same thing that helped me to find "me".

After my divorce I was still a pretty empty shell. I found a new home in my church family. My identity in Christ grew stronger than ever, but on a less spiritual level, there was still a part of myself that I was missing. I couldn't tell you when I had that eureka moment when it all came together but I do know how it came together. I had two very special people in my life at that time; my "coach" and my "diplomat". Like any good friend, they took the time to get to know me.

Now my friend, the diplomat (a silly, yet fitting nickname), would notice what my likes and dislikes were and he would mention them in casual conversation or include them in our plans. For example, some of the things I love and had forgotten about were waterfalls, stars, the beach and the color blue. There was one time in particular when he mentioned them all at once, and then some. He was trying to prove a point to say that he took great care to pay attention to people. Thank God someone did because it obviously wasn't me. I remember driving home that night in awe and I kept repeating to myself in a small whisper as if the truth was just hitting me, "My favorite color is blue." It was if I had found a treasure, a piece of a very important puzzle and I wasn't letting go.

My coach did the same for me. She was my pastor's wife and a spiritual parent, if you will. Only, I call her coach because a parent may go to a game and root for their child but it's a coach who will actually call a time-out to give you some much needed advice or pep talk. And when you win, it isn't just a third party win, it's their win too.

I remember Coach would always speak into my life. Sometimes they would be words of encouragement; God has something great for you, and other similar words of hope. But the most powerful words were the ones that reflected those things she already saw, almost like a list of facts. She would speak out what she saw in me or she would share what others had said. My favorite was when she would speak out the recent events that had taken place and share her amazement at God's hand in my life. The thing I loved about that was they were facts, plain and simple. There was no embellishing, no words for compliments sake that could easily be brushed aside as a pleasant nicety. They were undeniably true. And when something is undeniable you just have to accept it as truth. And it was those truths and encouragements that gave me the strength to become the woman I am today.

Today, I don't worry about "who I am". I am no longer in search of my identity. My identity is in Christ and the only thing I continue to seek is my purpose. And that seems to be a constantly changing thing. God's purpose for my life seems to change from one season to another. Although He is constantly doing a new work, ultimately that purpose is to be a vessel He can use for His glory, however He deems fit. Ultimately our identity is to be found in Christ, but that does not mean we need to neglect the search for self, so long as it's not to serve one's "self". We are fearfully and wonderfully made (Psalm 139:14) and I think that warrants some exploring. Besides, when discovering the creature you can't help but discover more about the Creator.

-7-
A Moment

Things have a funny way of coming full circle. Have
you ever had one of those moments that seem to freeze
time? That happened to me not too long ago. I was placed
in a situation where I had a very big decision to make. I was
the only one in the room who was even aware that anything
eventful was happening. Time seemed to be suspended as I
considered my next move, the pros, the cons and the
absurdity of it all. After all these years, it would come to this.
I literally had the opportunity of a lifetime. I had waited most
of 30 years wondering if and when I should share this secret
with the woman before me. And just the other day she
practically sets the scene up for the long awaited reveal, only
she couldn't possibly have known. It wouldn't even be as
awkward as I had pictured it when I played the scenario out
in my head. It would have been right on topic and with such
a smooth transition.

I came to visit this family member in the hospital while
they were recovering from a surgery. She was in the best of
spirits considering she had been in the hospital for ten days.
She was pleased with the success of the surgery and with
her speedy recovery. After some light hearted conversation,
her tone turned a bit serious. She was mentioning another
visitor she had earlier that week. She began to share with
me, that her visitor's son (a cousin of mine) had been
molested by her brother-in-law. Her son was now a grown

man but she hadn't found out about what happened to him until just recently. The offender had served time in prison for similar offenses to others. She just never knew that her son was also one of his victims.

The relative I was visiting was telling me I should be careful who I let my kids stay with. There was a single mom's retreat coming up at church that I was planning on going to. It would be my last opportunity to go on one, as I was soon to be married, so I really didn't want to miss it. Needless to say, I was on a mission to find a babysitter(s) for all four of my children. She was telling me that one could never really know who could be trusted, not even family.

She kept stressing the whole family issue, as if that connection was more offensive than the abuse itself. She must have read something in my expression because she asked, "Did I scare you? People forget that family members can do those things too." She thought I was worried about my children but my thoughts were actually elsewhere. I told her that I wasn't scared and I knew all too well the dangers of family. She thought I was referring to my ex husband and his abusive nature. But it wasn't my husband I was thinking of – it was hers.

It was her husband who had abused me as a child. I never said anything for… oh, about a gazillion reasons, most of which I could not explain. Actions made at such a young age are hard to rationalize but I will share a few thoughts that I remember having. First off, I knew that my dad would kill him. That was a one hundred percent given. Then I would end up with a dead relative, his heartbroken wife (both over his death and his crime), a father in prison and a mother left to deal with the rest of the fall out. Now those were some pretty serious thoughts and burdens to place on a young girl. It seemed silence was the lesser of two evils and so it was the path I chose.

Now, I wasn't a young child forever. There came a time, prior to this, when I would grow and be challenged again with "Do I tell or stay silent?" The decision making process went much the same only, it was slightly more complicated. At that time, I had seen such a transformation in the offender. By then he was serving God and the abuse had ended years earlier. It seemed unfair to tell now. Why wait until the man had straightened up his act, to ruin his life and the lives of those who loved him? At that time I would also hurt my siblings and cousins by ruining the relationships they grew to have with him as well. As a matter of fact, my brother even named his son after him – but as my former psychology professor word say, "that's a whole 'nuther Oprah." Everyone seemed to love this man and he was often the life of the party. No one suspected this man to have done harm to anyone, especially me, after all (insert red flag here), I was his "favorite". Yet I would have two more opportunities to bring the truth to the light. The next one began with a phone call.

It was the middle of the night. I was living with my parents at the time. The offender had been in the hospital for a few days after suffering a bout of congestive heart failure. I was in the living room, rocking my newborn to sleep after a feeding, when the phone rang. My mom and I must have picked up the phone at the same time but she spoke first, seemingly unaware that I was on the other line. Just as I moved to hang up the phone I heard a woman's voice on the other end telling my mother that my abuser had just passed away. I hung up the phone slowly as the meaning of those words began to sink in. I knew this person was a family member, loved by all, and that I should have felt very sad at the moment. But as I laid my head back on the rocker, I thought of the child I held in my arms, took a deep breath and felt relief rush out of my body, through every pore.

I felt so guilty for having such a heartless response. I could never have imagined feeling such an inappropriate emotion at the tragic ending of anyone's life. But I understood it all too well. There I was, shocked and confused by my thoughts. I felt as though God knew I needed to feel that my child to be safe and there was only one way that was going to happen. I know that's not why he passed away and yet those were my thoughts and in all my humanness I believed God's timing to be very appropriate. He lived to see my firstborn child (a gift I believe, for his repentant life) but he died just one month after her birth, granting me a sense of peace and closure; something I didn't even know I needed until that moment. It was as if I was holding my breath from the moment my child was born and I needed someone to give me a good slap and say, "Breathe!"

You would think that maybe then would have been a good time to share my ugly secret with someone. I would no longer have to worry about hurting him as he tried to live the remainder of his life as best he could. But it was almost worse. Now I had his memory to contend with. These people who loved and lost him would hate me for defiling their memory of him. I would be taking away the only thing they had left. Why after all these years would I choose to say something now? It would be a hateful thing, not to mention, pointless. The only one it would help was me. The truth would not hold him accountable and it would not protect anyone else. No, the truth would only bring harm. It seemed to me that at every turn the truth was harmful… and I kept waiting for it to set me free.

But here I was, in a hospital room with the woman who could help me do just that. She was so upset over a family member abusing another family member. She was asking me if I was worried about something like that happening. It would have been an easy transition to say, "Actually I know exactly what it's like. I've never told anyone because I didn't want anyone to get hurt. But maybe now is the time I shared something with you…" I could have approached it gently and tactfully. But as time continued to pause and thoughts continued to fly by, I realized I simply couldn't do that because it would be unfair to her.

She was well into the last half of her years on this earth, widowed for the past twelve, comforted only by telling stories to my children of her adventures with her husband. I couldn't take that away from her any more than I could stop my internal eyes from rolling every time I heard his name and how wonderful he was. It also wouldn't be fair to her because the news would leave her helpless. Had I told her sooner, she would have had the opportunity to react, to respond, to walk away, to do something or *anything*. To tell her now would leave her powerless, feeling like she had failed her family and did not protect them from harm. Instead of reminiscing about the good old days she would be haunted by thoughts of what happened and what she could have done differently to prevent it and other horrible thoughts like "I should have known," etc. So, I looked her in the eyes and gave a vague answer followed by a silence she would never recognize… and time was once again in flow.

It wasn't a frustrating decision to make this time. I felt in complete control and somewhat empowered, as if I had been offered something I had been waiting for, only to refuse it for something I thought was needed much more. And oddly enough that was all the freedom I needed. Now *that's* what you call a moment.

-8-
Before the Ink Runs Dry

There are certain things that I would clear up before these chapters come to a close. Although this book has shared with you some events that I have experienced, it is hardly the story of my life. As a matter of fact, friends have questioned me, what about (*this?*) and what about (*that?*) in regards to some very profound moments in my life that have followed in the years since the time period I touched upon in this book. It wasn't meant to be an all encompassing biography. It's just a book meant to address the whole double-agent factor; a clear message that says God is God and His message is worth holding on to no matter how you received it.

The hope He's given you, the faith that has bloomed within you is yours and no one else's. You own that relationship with your Creator and no one can take it away! I was also aware as I wrote these pages that many of them were filled with very bleak events, as though I had lived under a shadow of sorts. But it was just the opposite. You see, the Light of Jesus can and will outshine any darkness and that is the true message of this book.

Don't drown in choppy waters because the guy throwing the life preserver was the mean fellow who stole your seat when you first boarded the boat. Focus on what can save you, not on what caused you pain because that could end up costing you your life.   And if its eternity on the other end of that rope – you better grab hold! I wish I could tell you that everyone who shares the Gospel is good but I can't. There is no one good but God (Mark 10:18). Just learn to focus in on the Master and not the messenger – don't lose out on a relationship with your Creator because of a sour relationship here on Earth.

I've heard many people complain and even turn from God because of hurts done to them by Christians. I've seen pastors lose their faith because of hurts done to them by others as well. I've seen congregations give up their faith when they had given up on their pastors. When will we learn that God is God and man is man? We are responsible for the testimony we leave behind but we are also responsible for our excuses as to why we reject God.

We make mistakes and we live with the consequences of those mistakes. But guess what? God walks right alongside us the whole way. And He sets those paths straight. God hasn't changed. He is the same yesterday, today and forever (Hebrews 13:8) – isn't that worth holding on to? It was for me – through both the good times and the bad times.

I was blessed with the opportunity to experience some amazing times in ministry as a missionary and a pastor's wife (when things were good) and then I learned to struggle through the trials that tested the very foundation of my faith (when things were not so good). Through it all, I learned that even when man fails you, God is forever true and faithful (1 Corinthians 1:9). His promises are even greater than we imagine them to be.

Now, as for the events and hurts that I have shared in this book, not only are they not burdens that I have carried with me everyday since but they also feel as though they are a lifetime away from being a lifetime away. That's how great and mighty God is. So let us have compassion for others out there who have been hurt by people so much that they are calloused to God's message. A word of caution, if you don't have a heart for the lost, you may just be losing heart. So pray for those who are lost because God's Word has the power to transform lives and if He could take me from such a broken and hopeless place to a place of such overwhelming joy – just imagine what He can do for them – including your loved ones!

Life is exciting; everyday is such an amazing journey with God… I wake up excited just waiting to see what God has planned next. In fact, I have trouble sleeping because I'm so excited. I suppose that's how this book was born in the first place. I cannot think of a single thing right now that I have wanted to do that I have not had the opportunity to accomplish.

God has opened so many doors it's incredible… and He keeps opening them. We just need to pay attention, keep in step with the Spirit, and walk in boldness. Sometimes exciting can also be scary and intimidating but if we walk in the confidence of the Lord, He will do the rest. He just needs a people who are willing and available. "Here am I. Send me" (Isaiah 6:8).

Contact the author at: jbingham.pfs@gmail.com

Scripture References (NKJV)

(http://www.blueletterbible.org)

<u>Introduction - My Race to the Starting Line</u>

Philippians 3:14
I press toward the goal for the prize of the upward call of
God in Christ Jesus.

Philippians 1:6
being confident of this very thing, that He who has begun a
good work in you will complete it until the day of Jesus
Christ;

Romans 8:37
Yet in all these things we are more than conquerors through
Him who loved us.

1 John 5:4
For whatever is born of God overcomes the world. And this
is the victory that has overcome the world—our faith.

Hebrews 12: 1
Therefore we also, since we are surrounded by so great a
cloud of witnesses, let us lay aside every weight, and the sin
which so easily ensnares us, and let us run with endurance
the race that is set before us,

<u>Chapter 1 - The Treasure in the Testimony I Fail to Share…
(until now)</u>

Romans 8:28
And we know that all things work together for good to those
who love God, to those who are the called according to His
purpose.

John 8:36
Therefore if the Son makes you free, you shall be free
indeed.

1 Corinthians 14:33a
For God is not the author of confusion but of peace, as in all
the churches of the saints.

2 Timothy 1:7
For God has not given us a spirit of fear, but of power and of
love and of a sound mind.

Psalm 4:8
I will both lie down in peace, and sleep; For You alone, O
LORD, make me dwell in safety.

James 4:8a
Draw near to God and He will draw near to you.

Jeremiah 29:11
For I know the thoughts that I think toward you, says the
LORD, thoughts of peace and not of evil, to give you a future
and a hope.

Chapter 2 – A Thousand Reasons and None

Psalm 37:4
Delight yourself also in the LORD, And He shall give you the
desires of your heart..

Psalm 5:12
For You, O LORD, will bless the righteous; With favor You
will surround him as with a shield.

Proverbs 12:2
A good man obtains favor from the LORD, But a man of wicked intentions He will condemn.

Chapter 3 – The Negotiating Room

1 Samuel Chapters 8-12

Chapter 4 – Following the Leader

Psalm 144:1
A Psalm of David. Blessed [be] the LORD my Rock, Who trains my hands for war, [And] my fingers for battle—

Mark 9:24
Immediately the father of the child cried out and said with tears, "Lord, I believe; help my unbelief!"

Chapter 5 – No U-Turns Allowed

Hebrews 13:5b
For He Himself has said, "I will never leave you nor forsake you."

Joshua 1:9
Have I not commanded you? Be strong and of good courage; do not be afraid, nor be dismayed, for the LORD your God is with you wherever you go."

Chapter 6 – You Complete Me

Psalm 139:14
I will praise You, for I am fearfully and wonderfully made; Marvelous are Your works, And that my soul knows very well.

Mark 10:18
So Jesus said to him, "Why do you call Me good? No one is good but One, that is, God.

Hebrews 13:8
Jesus Christ [is] the same yesterday, today, and forever.

Corinthians 1:9
God is faithful, by whom you were called into the fellowship of His Son, Jesus Christ our Lord.

Isaiah 6:8
Also I heard the voice of the Lord, saying: "Whom shall I send, And who will go for Us?" Then I said, "Here am I! Send me."

Coming Soon...

Focused
on the
Master
Not the Messenger

Companion Book for Individual
or Small Group Studies

Don't Forget to Check Out
Our Children's Books
With a Godly Message!

And more...

- Don't Pack Your Clothes in an Elephant's Trunk!
- Socks with Ruffles
- Finley Chronicles: A Sticky Situation
- Faith, Hope & Love
- Rotten Randy

Proudly Presents...

Sheila R. Cone
(https://www.facebook.com/SheilaRCone)

Sheila is the author of "The Book of Remembrance" and "The Everlasting", with the third book of this epic fantasy trilogy soon to follow (In the Beginning). The characters and settings in these books draw you immediately into a lush world full of shrouded mystery. The characters enamor you immediately and keep you coming back for more… and Sheila has graciously indulged our cravings!

The Book of Remembrance

As Rayniann anguishes over his life in a small village, a stranger reveals truths that set him on a wild conquest to discover his destiny.

What if your bloodline came from a race of supernatural beings, and you didn't know it? Would you seek to find the answers, or would you let the decay of the village mold your life? These are the questions Rayniann must resolve in The Book of Remembrance, when a stranger arrives in his village and begins to tell him things he can't quite comprehend.

At the moment of the stranger's arrival he is broken over the death of his mother, but he questions whether her death was accidental or planned. An unexpected betrayal from someone his mother trusted puts Rayniann in the middle of a wild conquest, with the stranger as his guide.

As he battles a barrage of dark enemies and his own fears, Rayniann falls in love with a woman whose own brokenness helps him to embrace the truth. He begins to understand that his life comprises of he not only freeing the world of the darkness that consumes it, but freeing his own soul from the misery of mankind's destruction. Rayniann's discovery of truth leads him to one single purpose, but will he have the strength to accept the sacrifice?

ISBN: 978-0615598925
(https://www.facebook.com/bookofremembrance)

Made in the USA
Charleston, SC
02 July 2015